Copyright © 2020 Math Art Publishing
All rights reserved. This book or any portion thereof
may not be reproduced or used in any manner whatsoever
without the express written permission of the publisher.

DEDICATION

"Here's to when Mathematics and Art come together!"

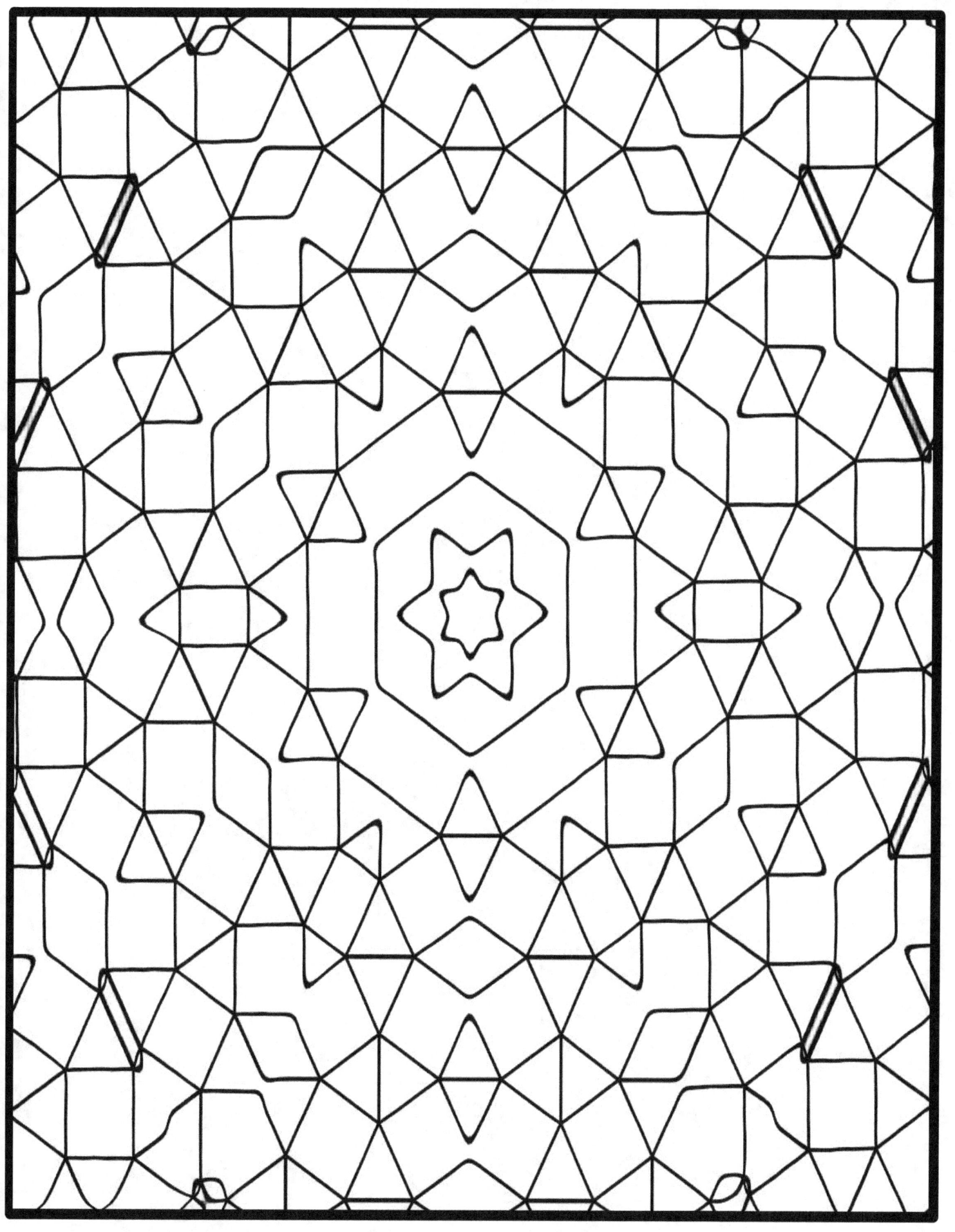

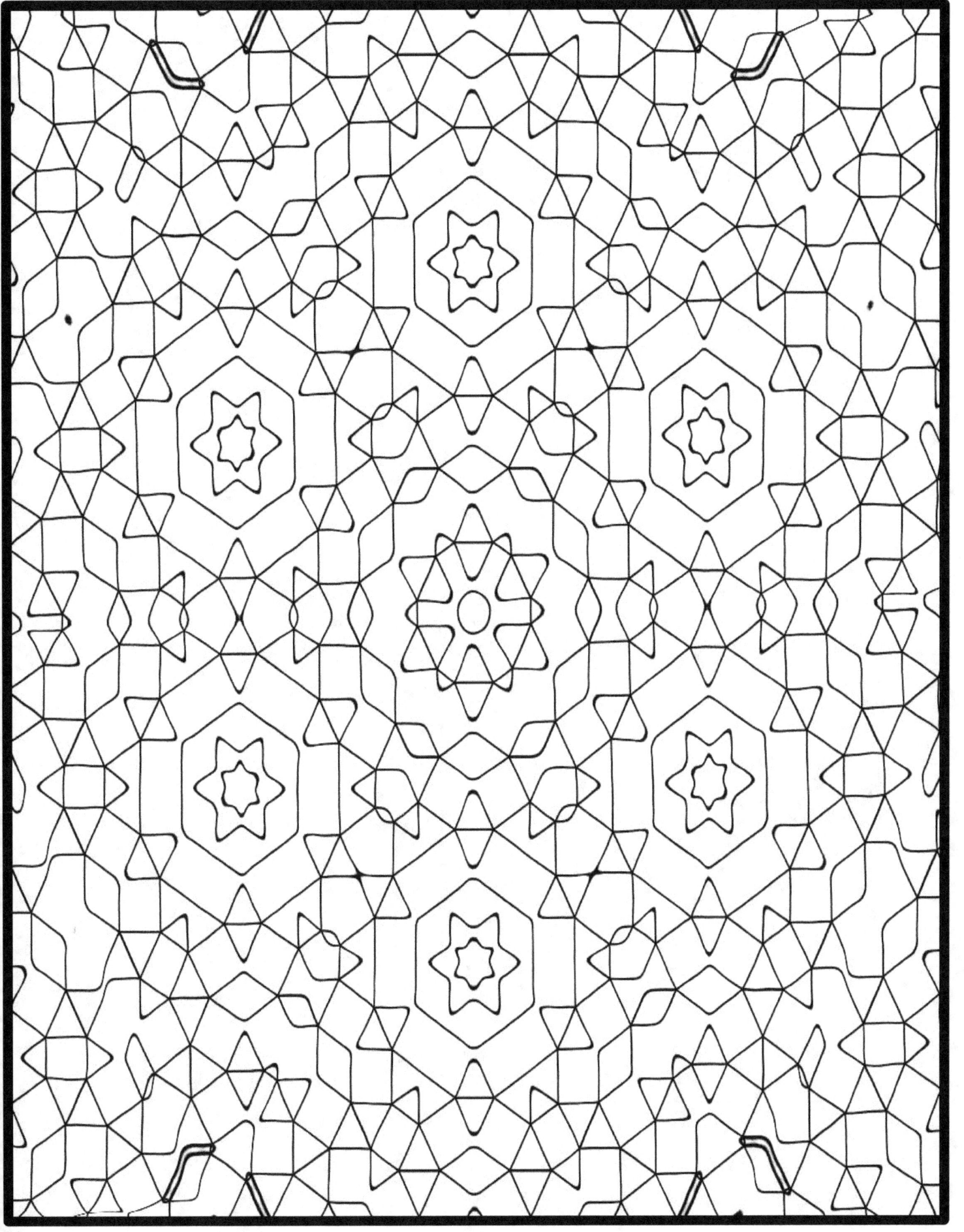

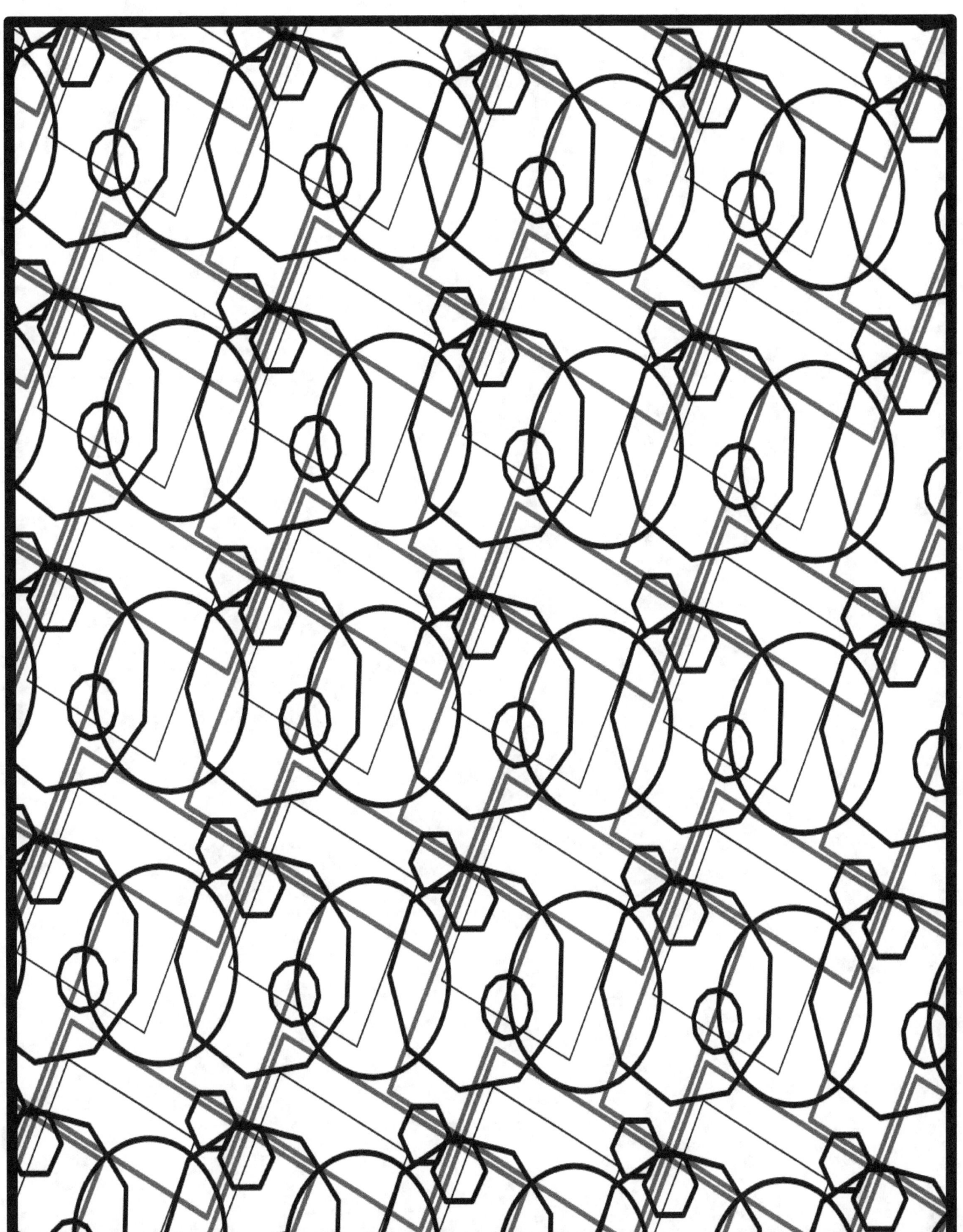

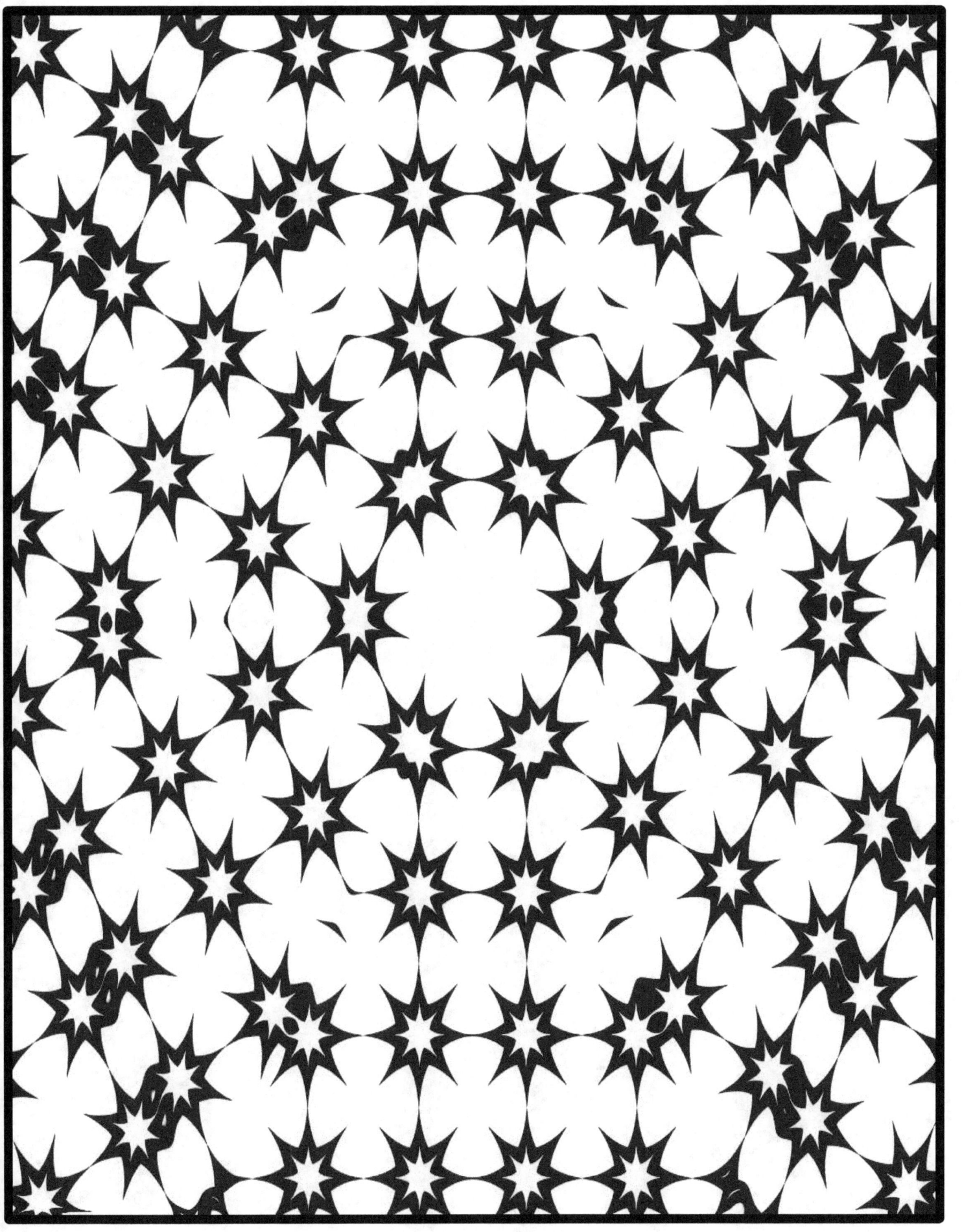

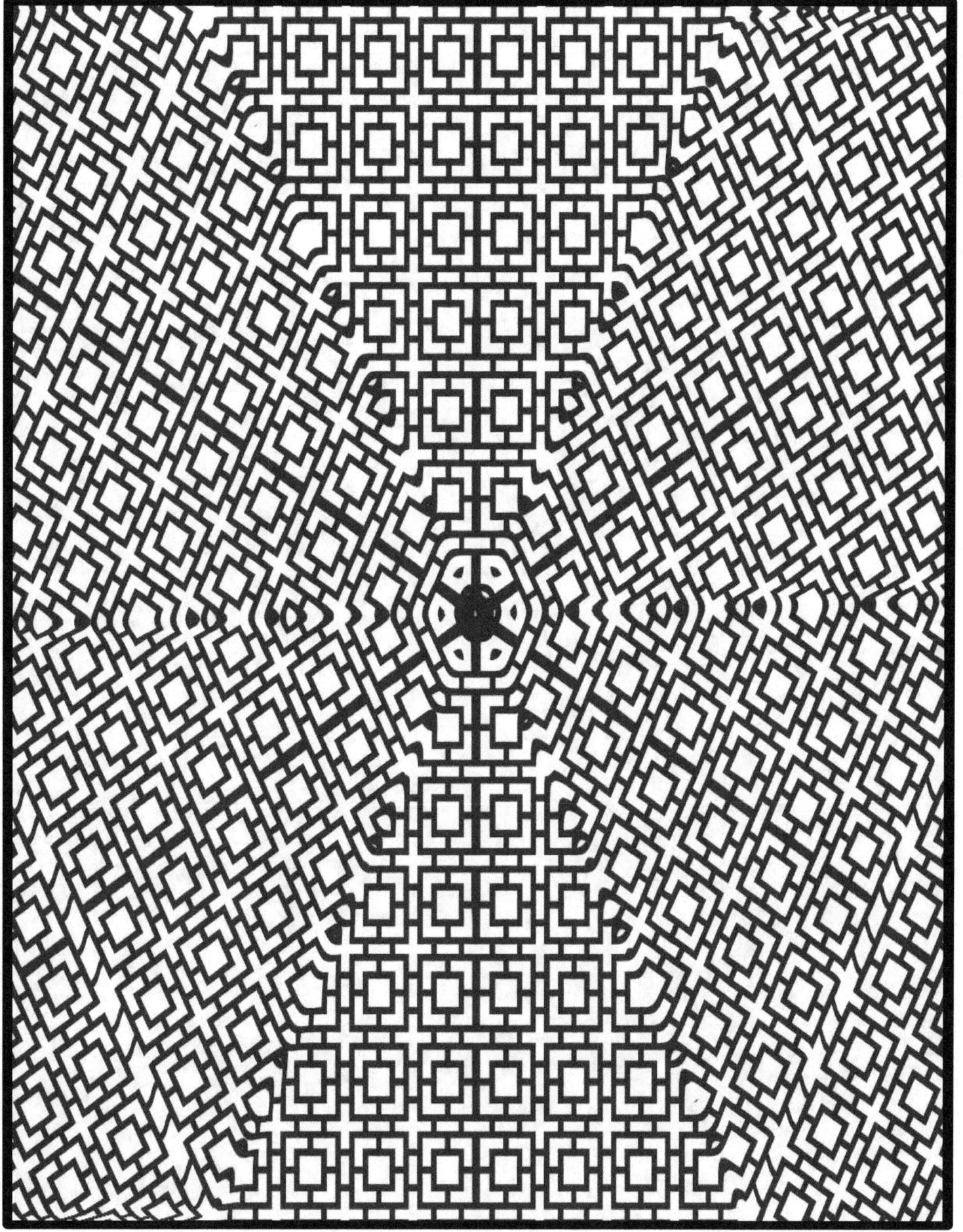

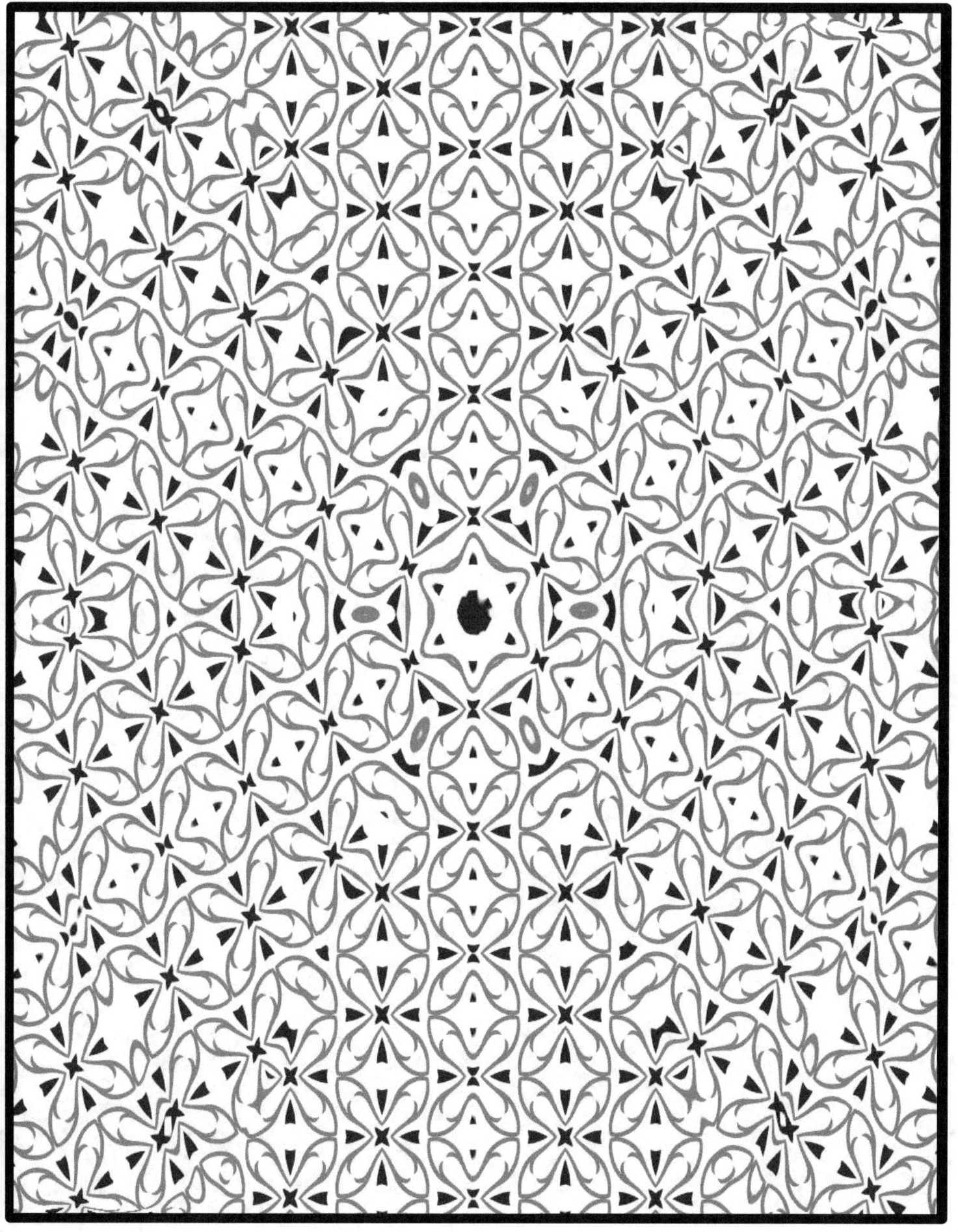

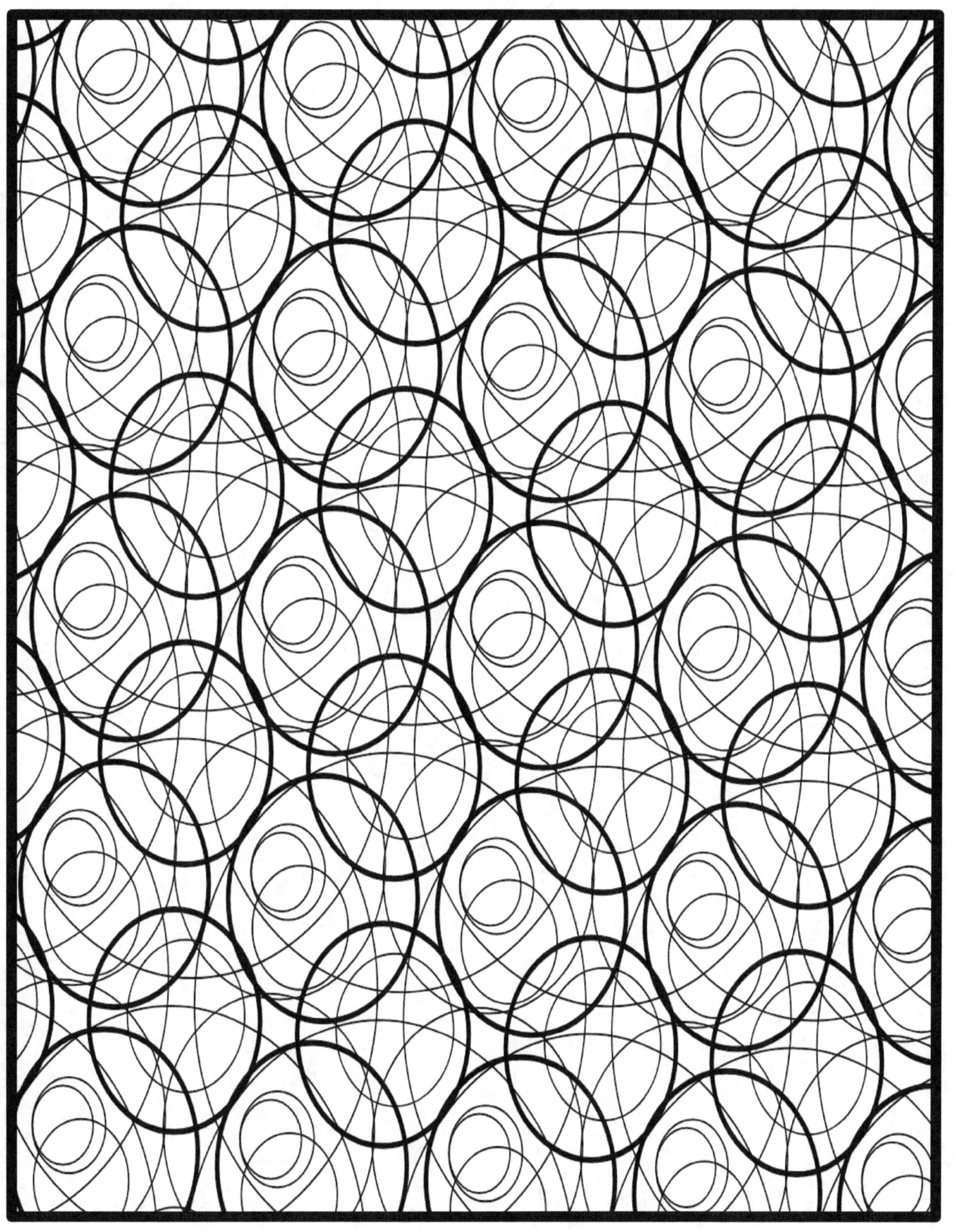

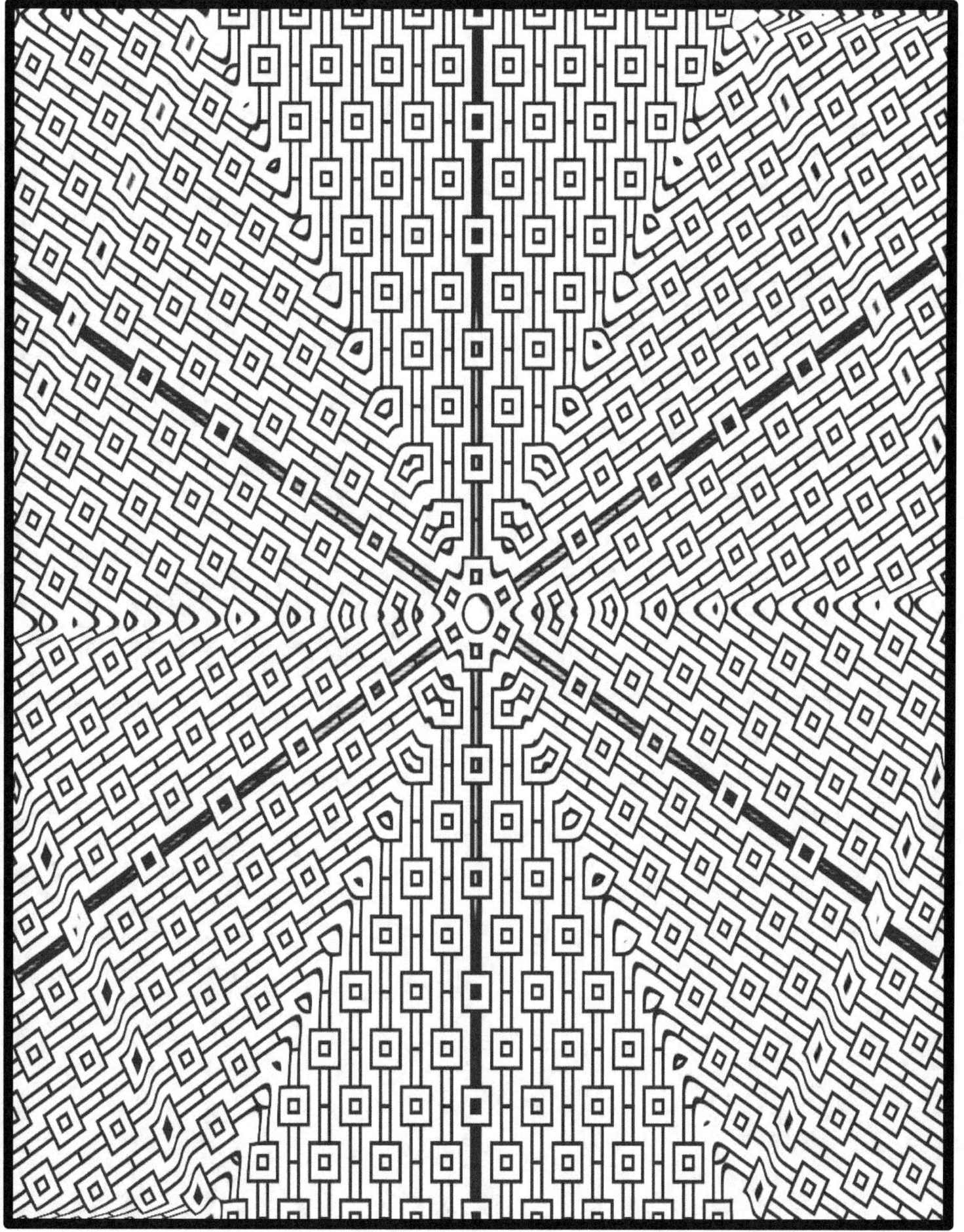

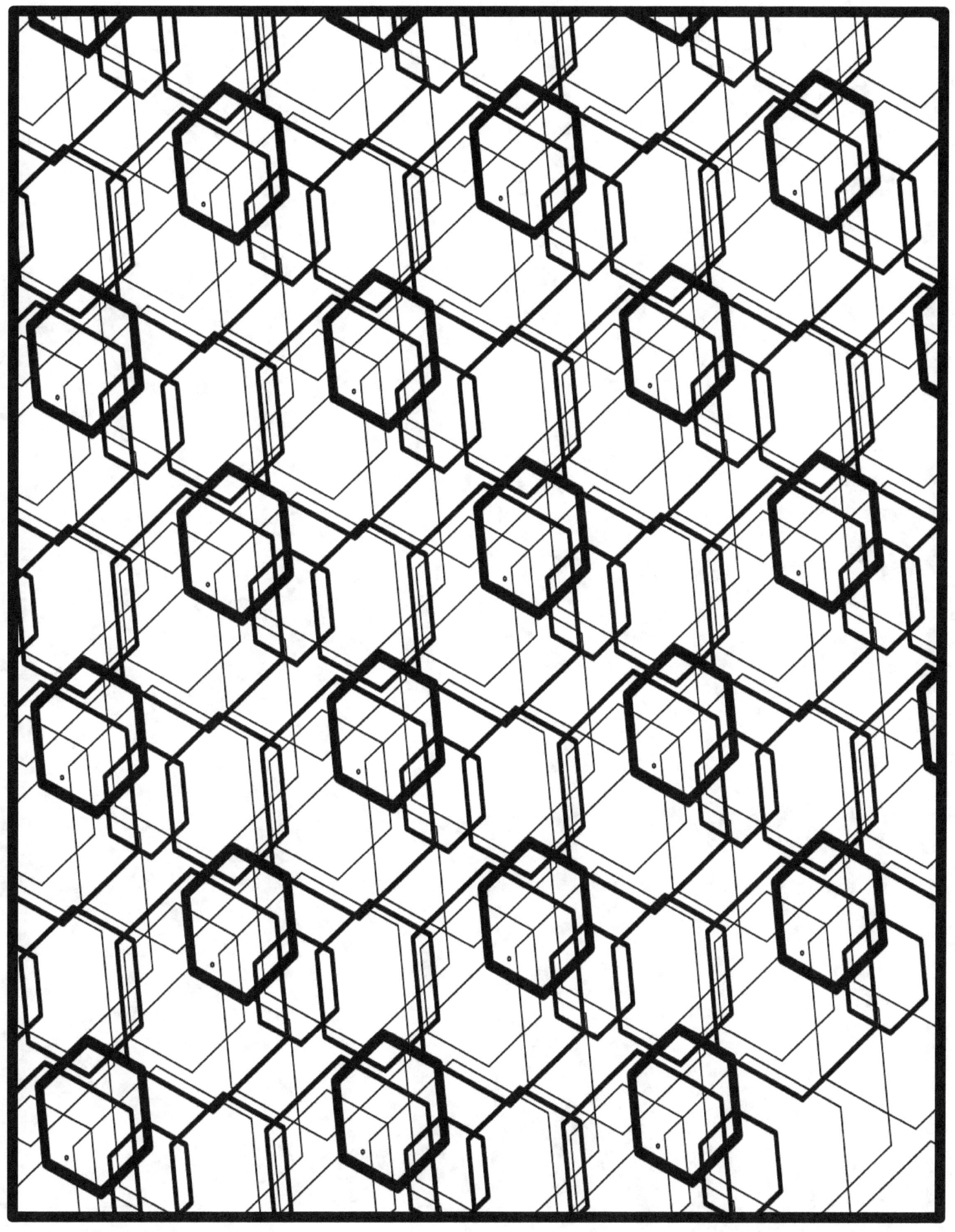

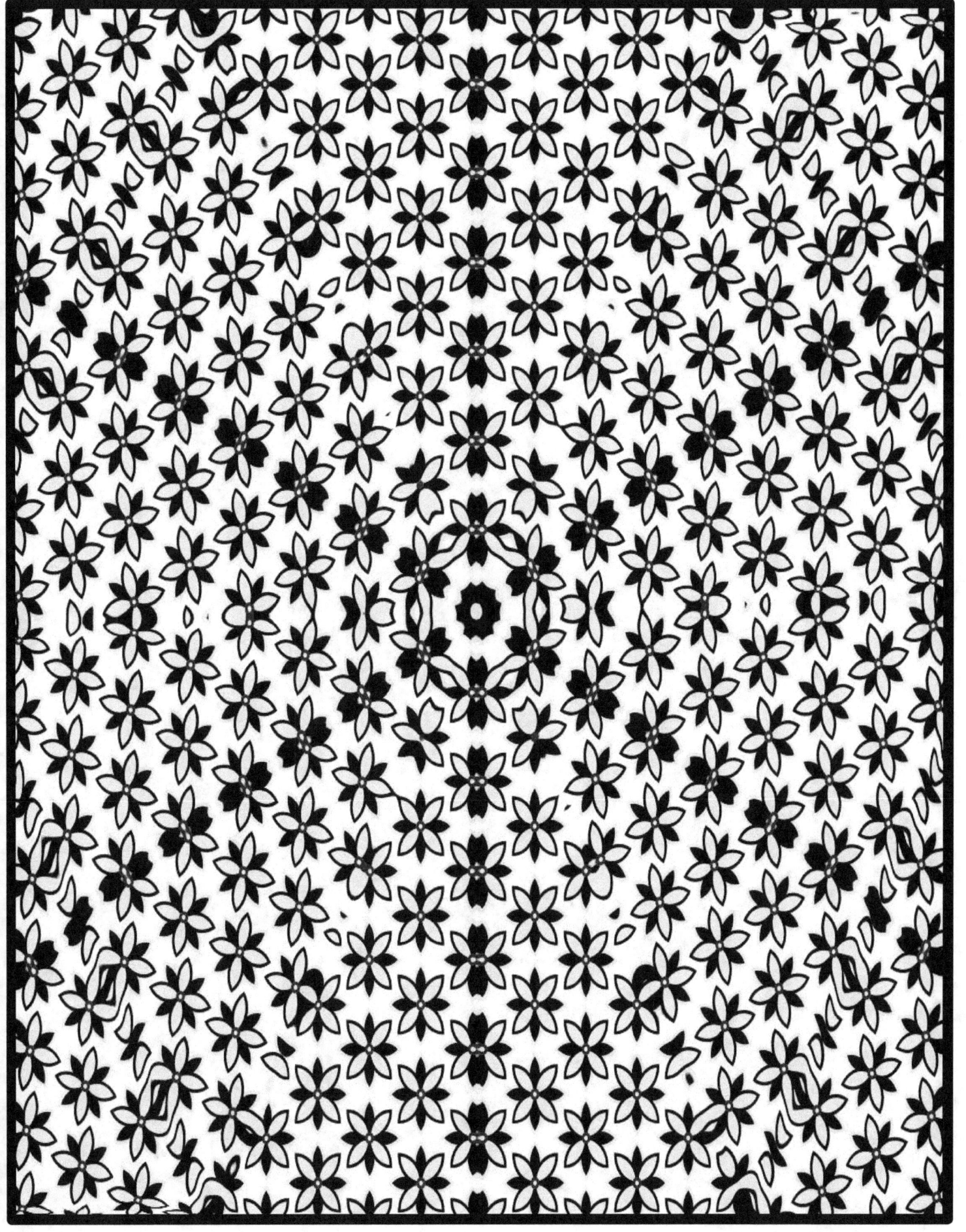

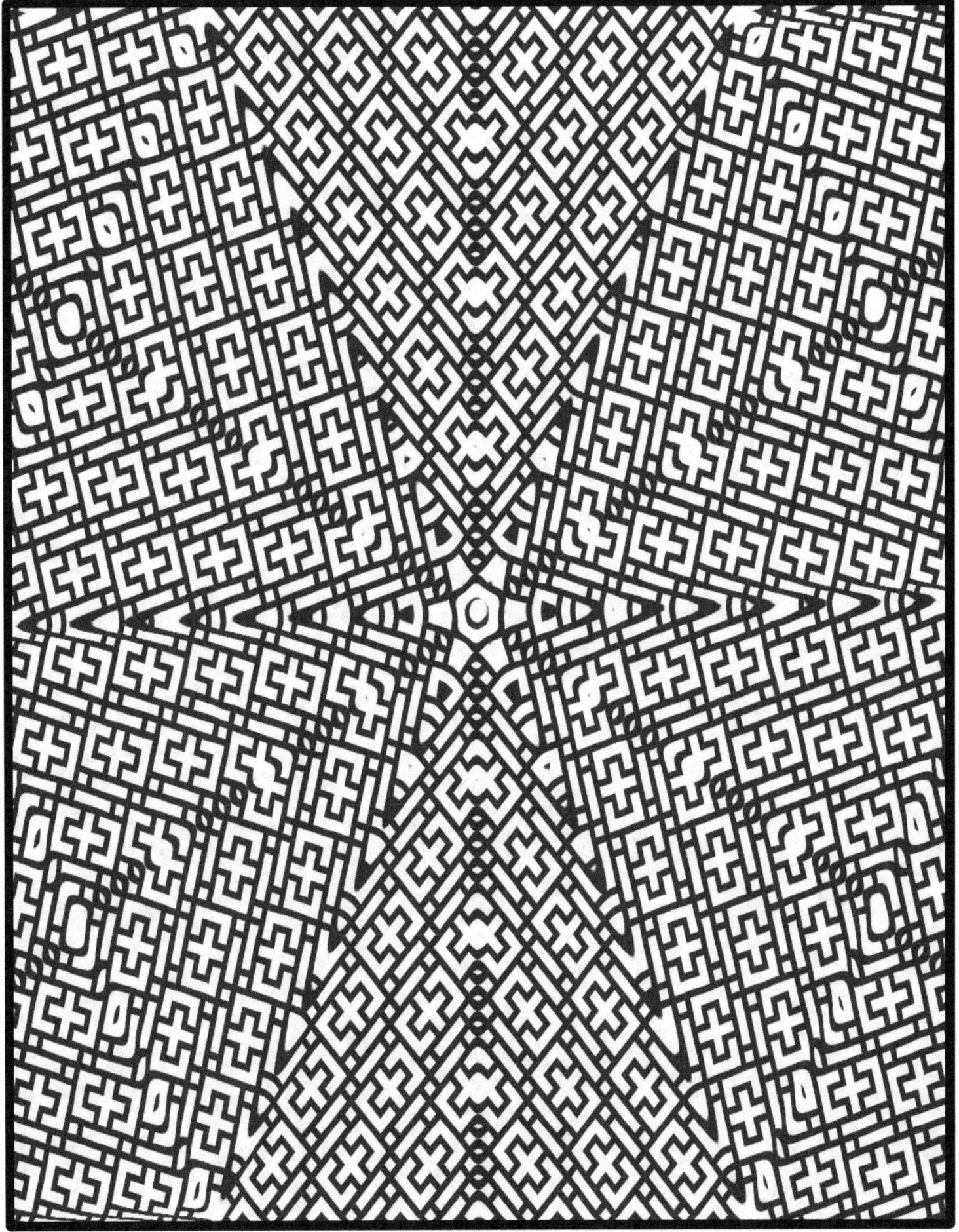

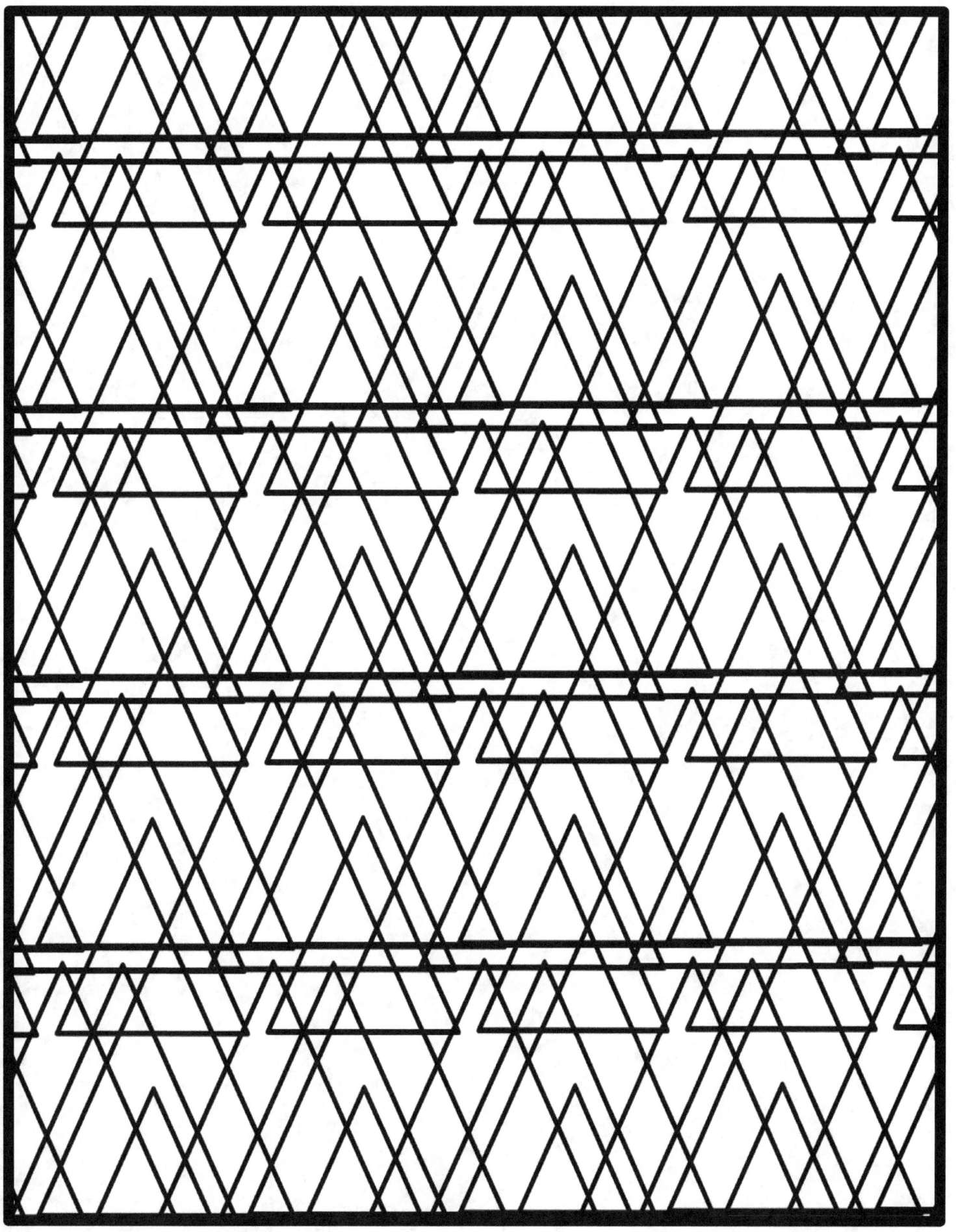

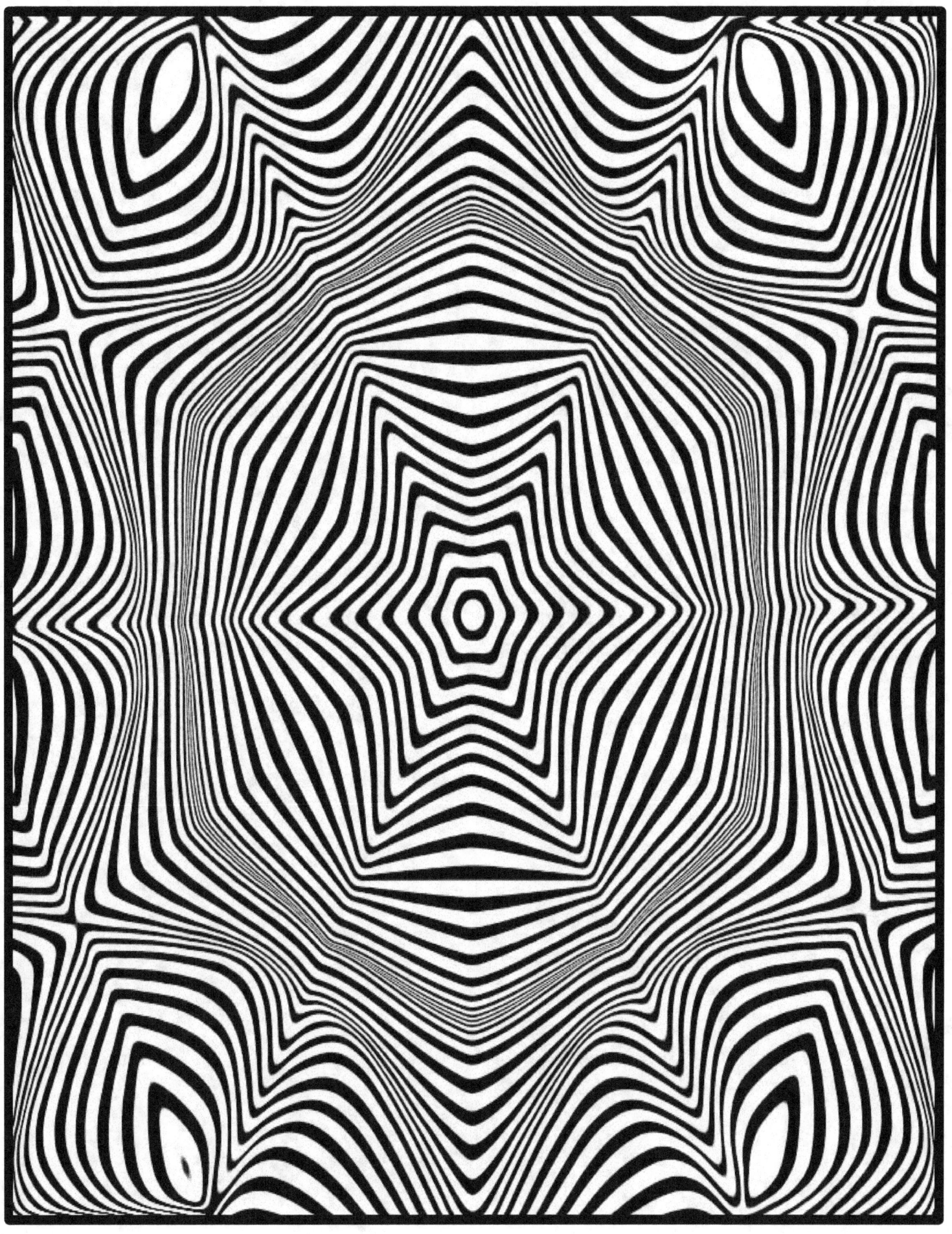

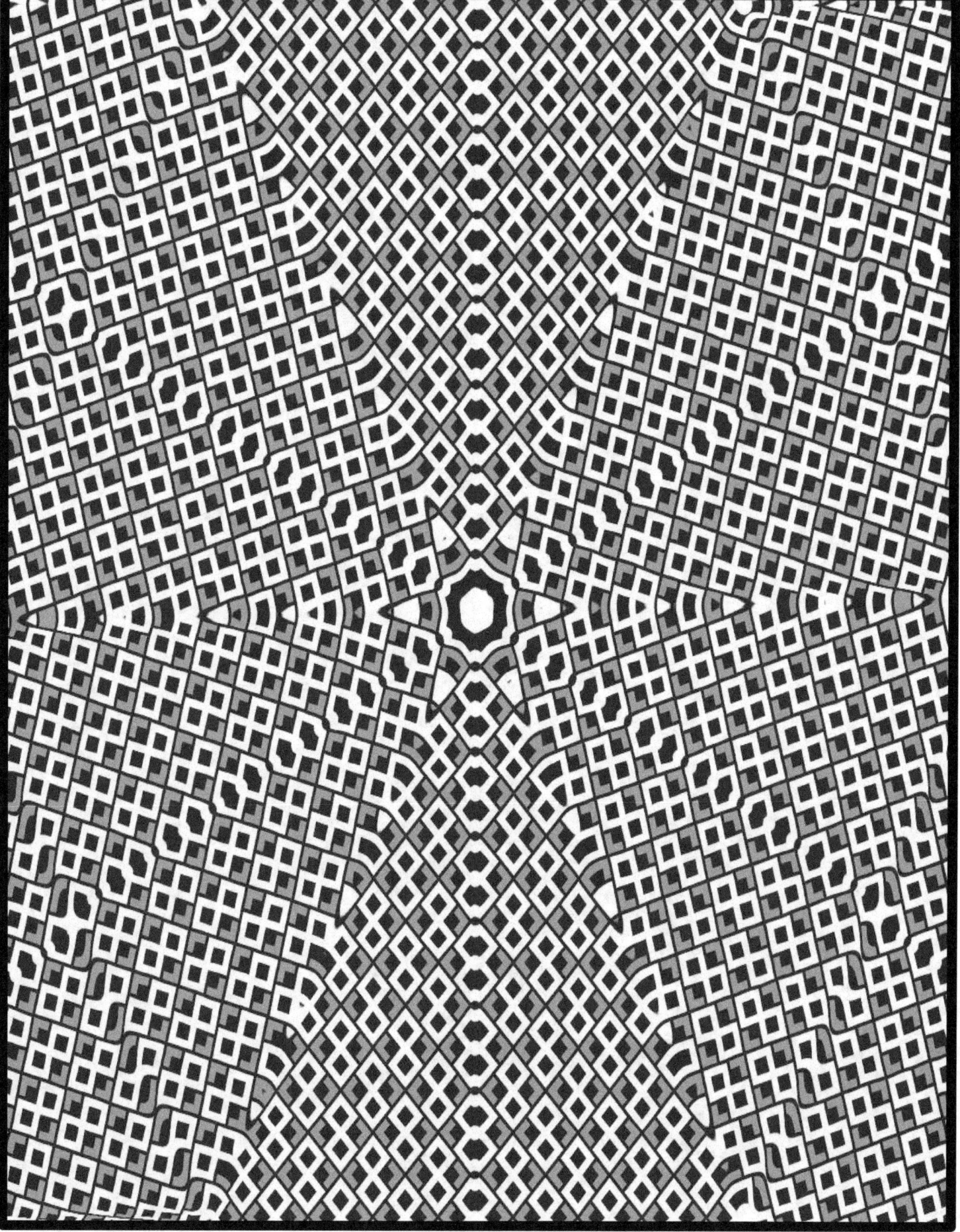

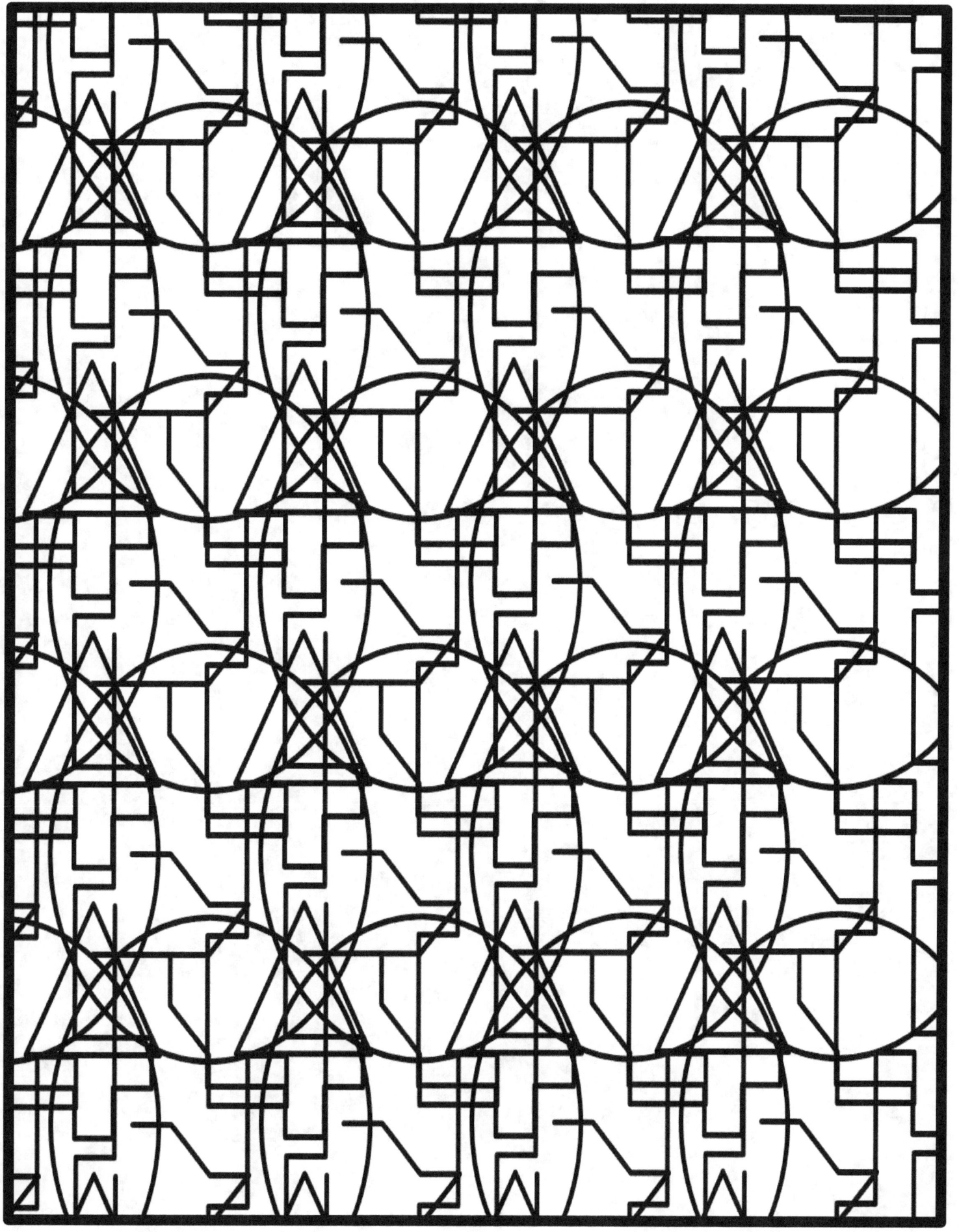

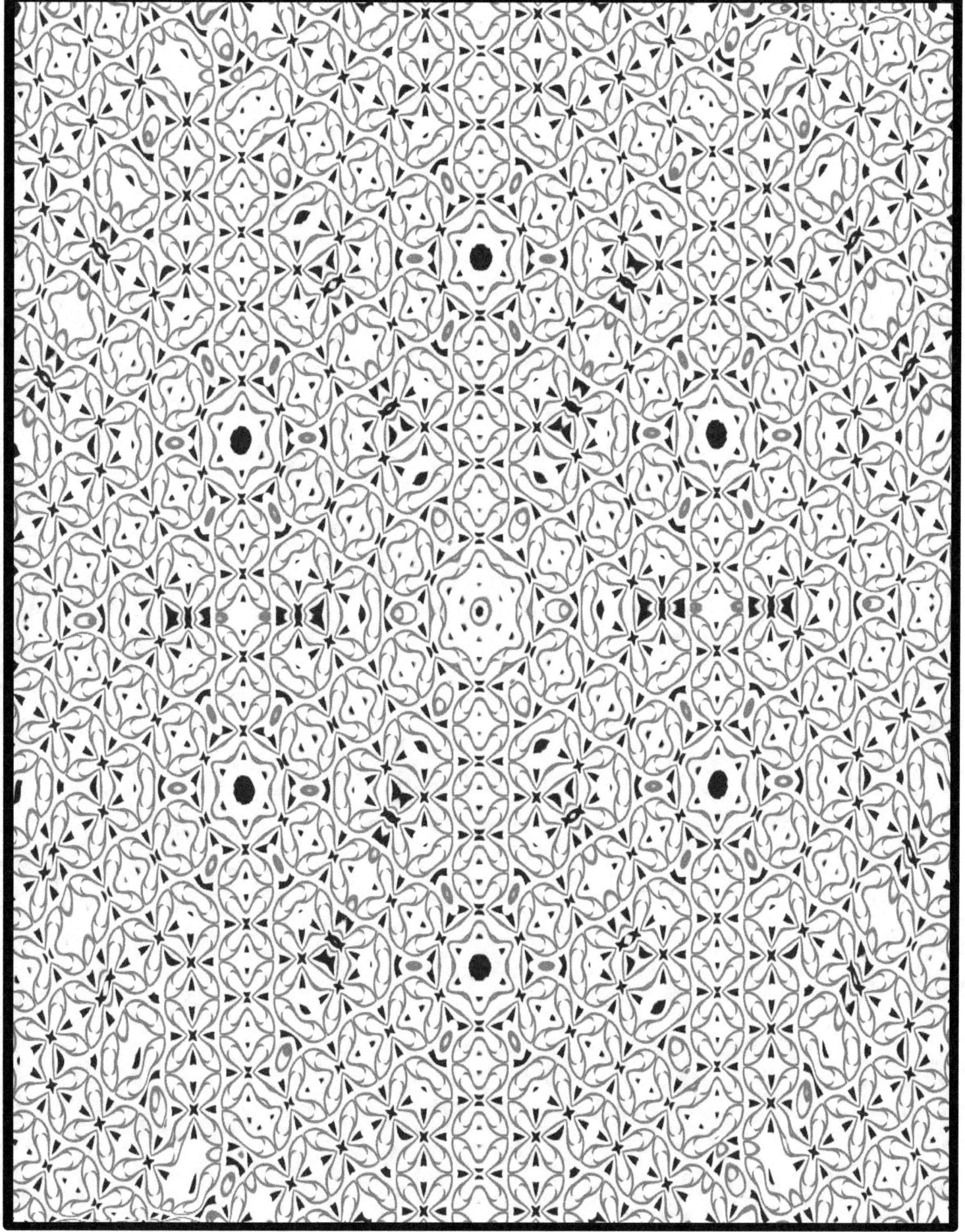

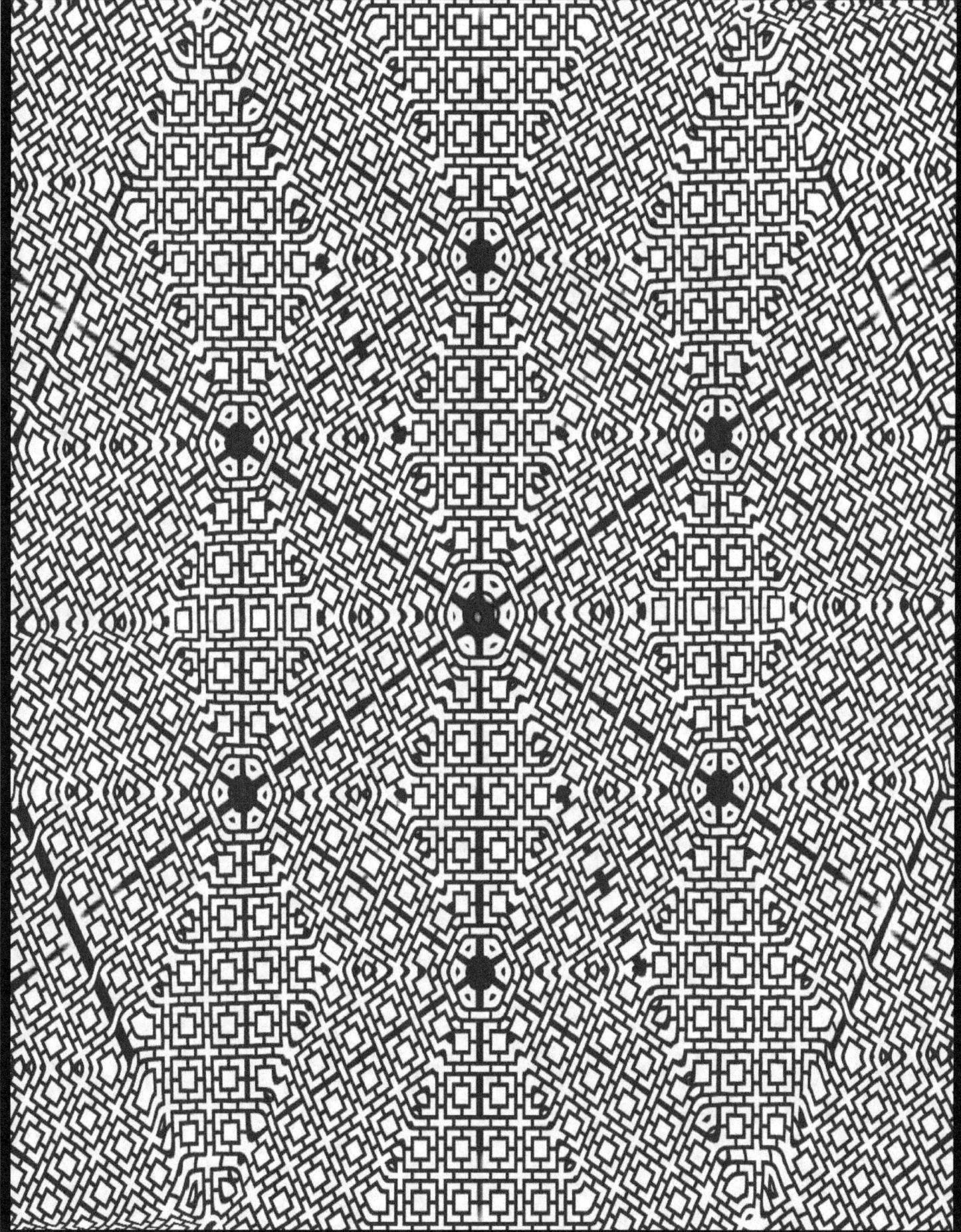

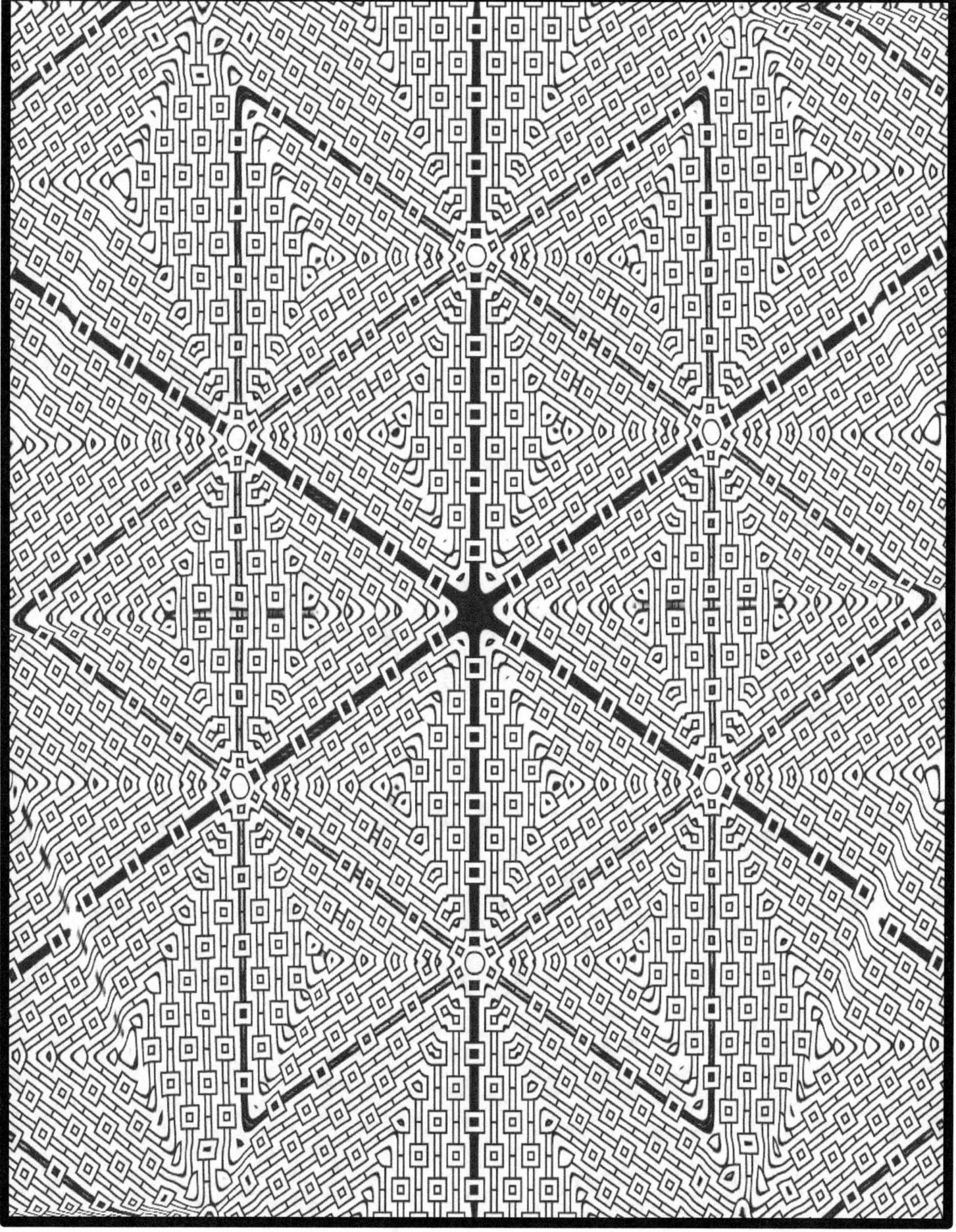

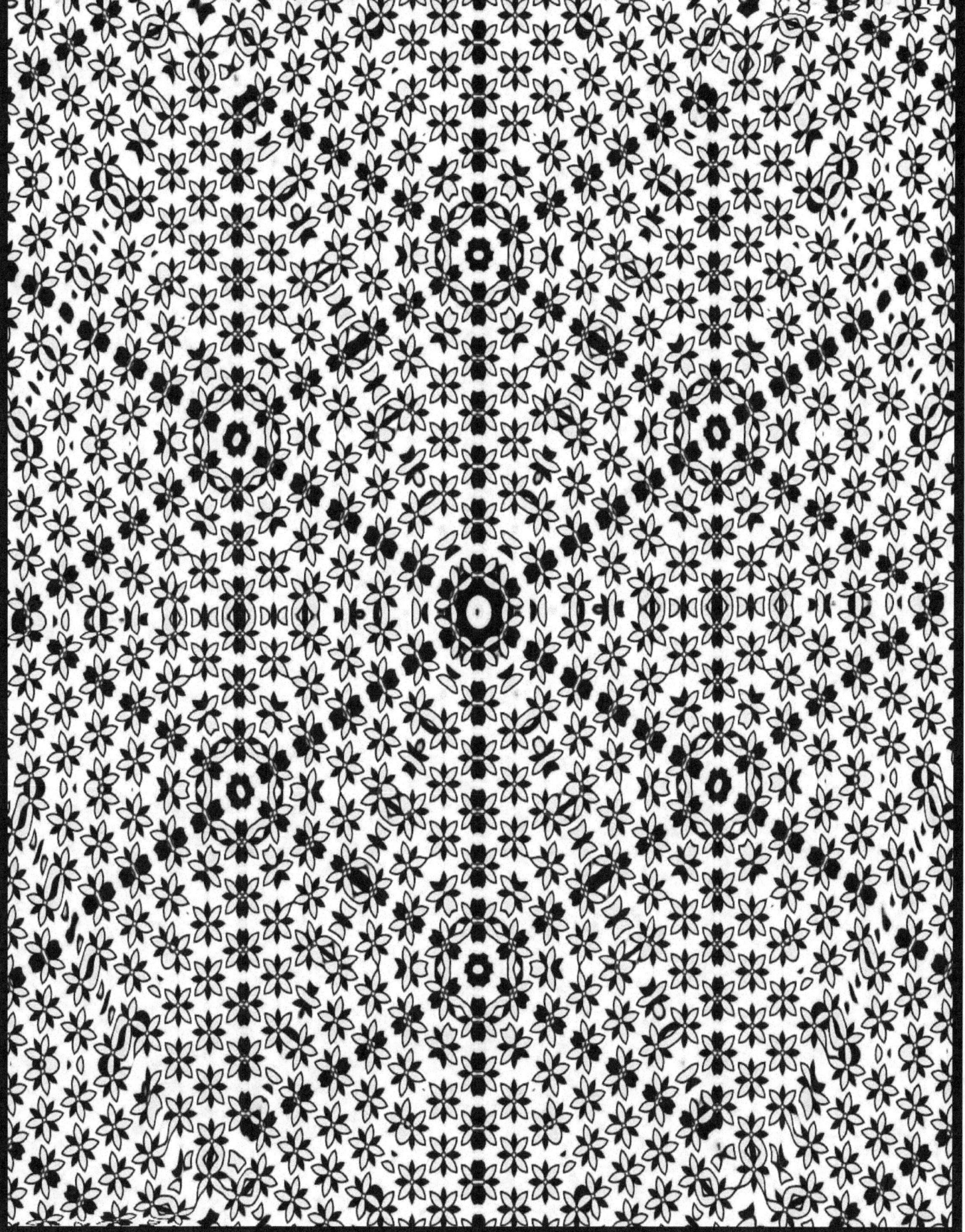

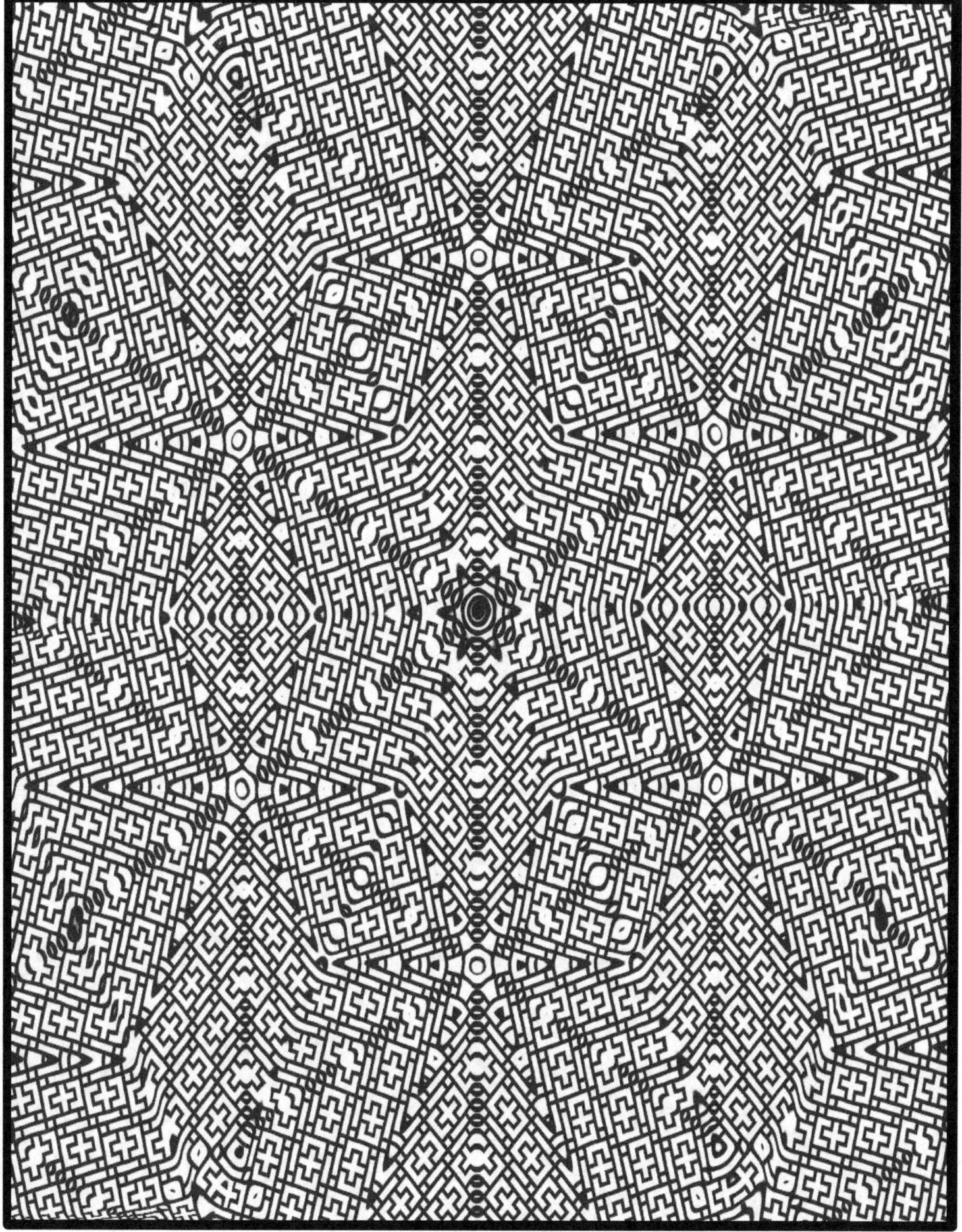

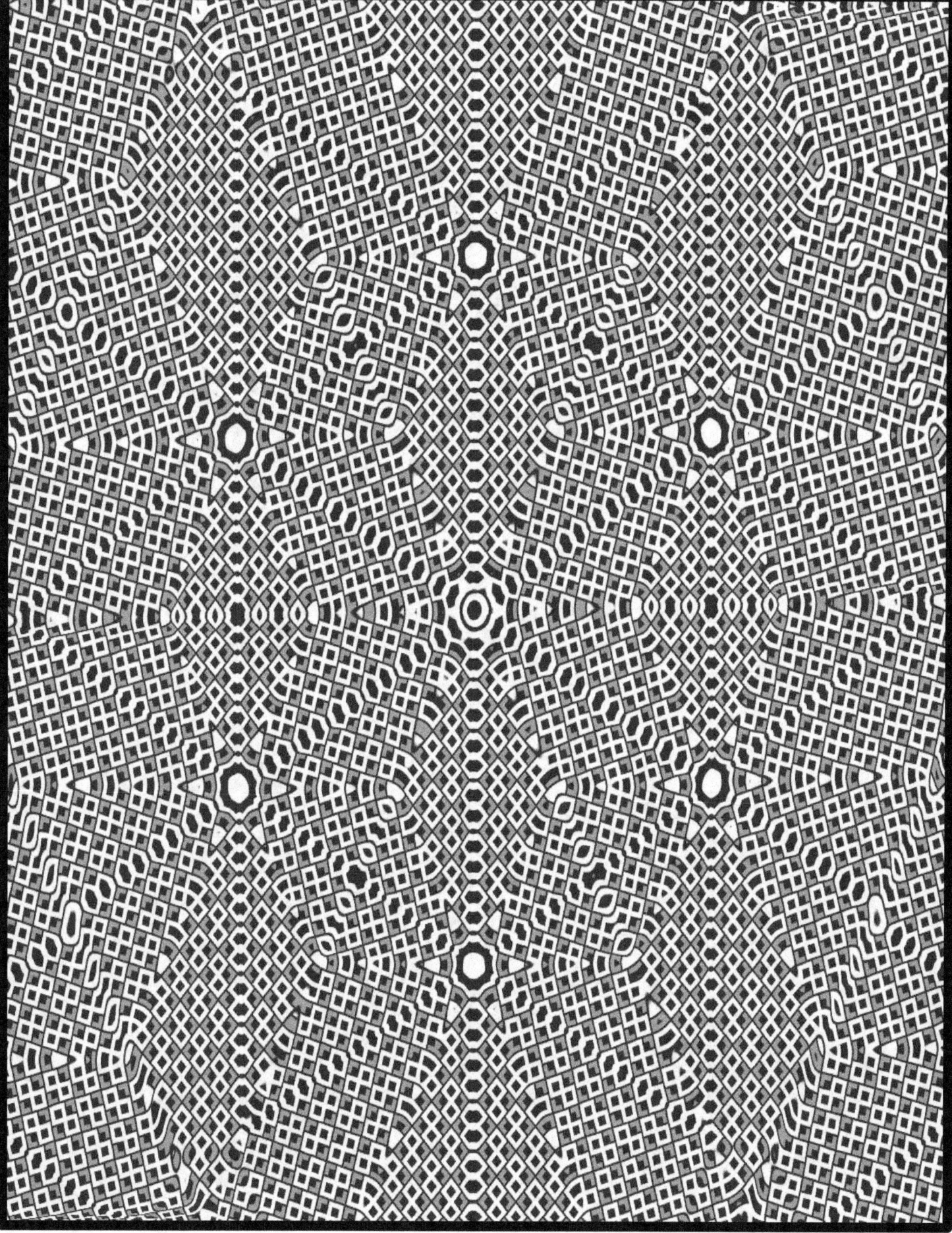

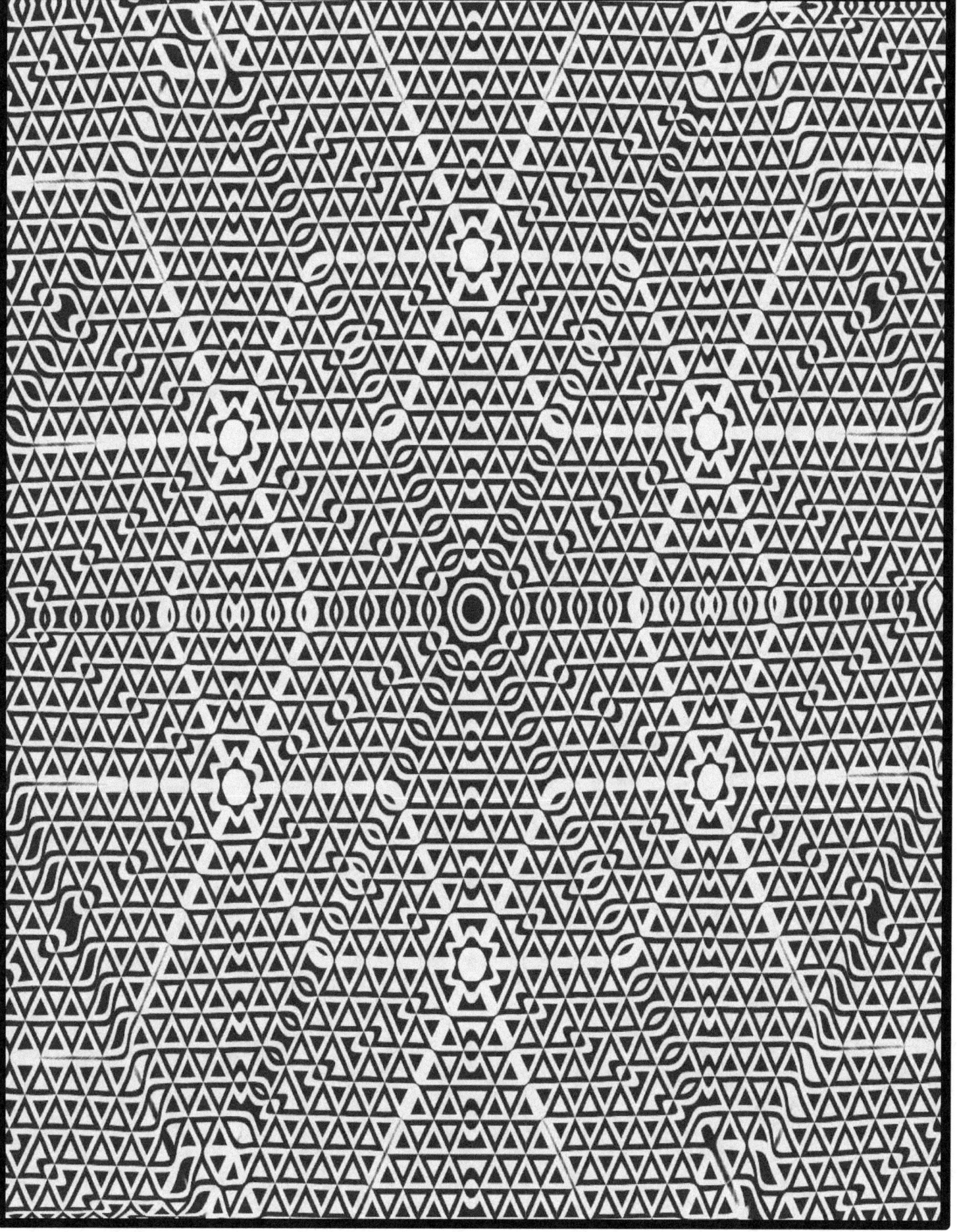

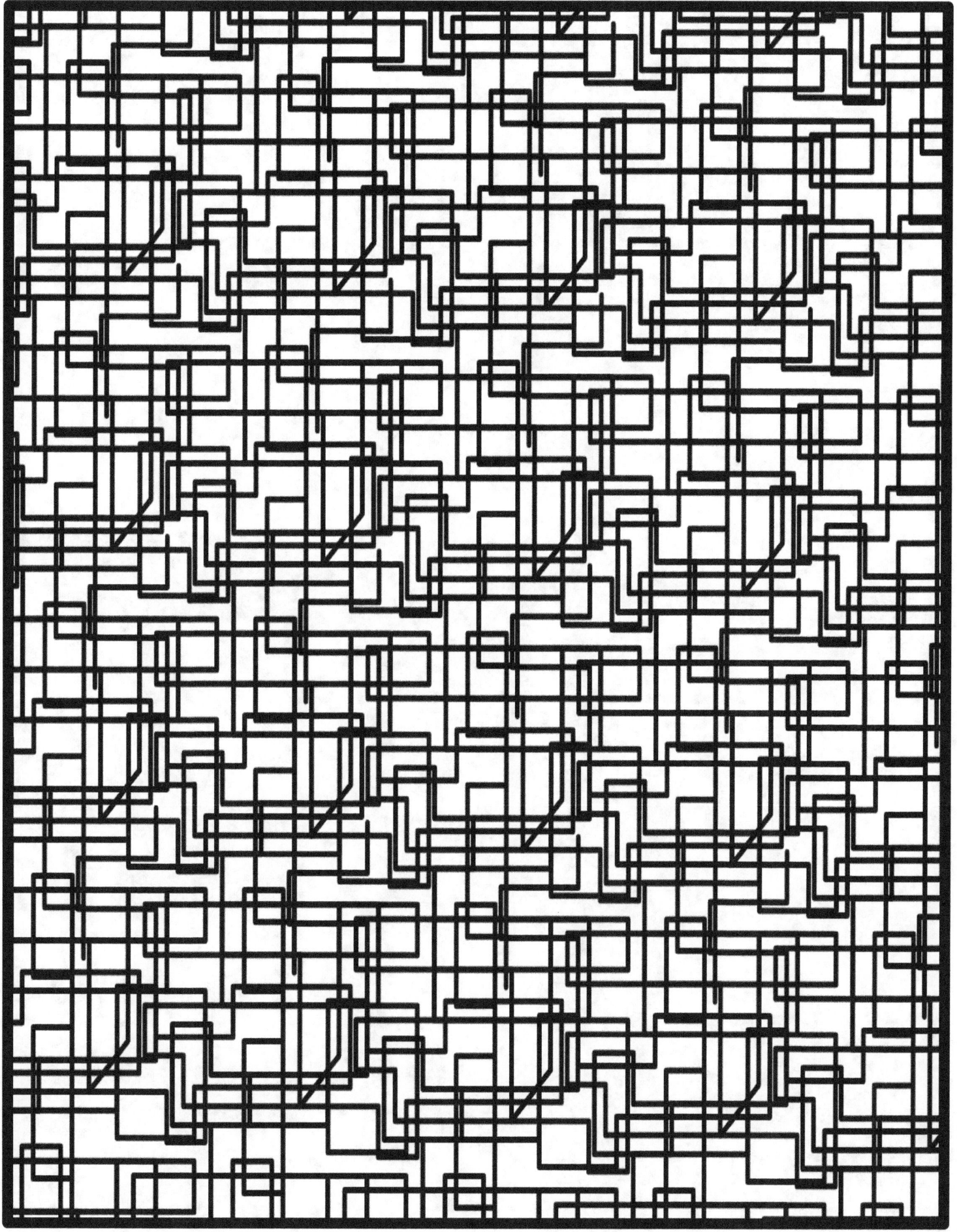

www.ingramcontent.com/pod-product-compliance
Lightning Source LLC
Chambersburg PA
CBHW081703220526
45466CB00009B/2863

9 781655 641466